W9-DDE-401

# Gettysburg

## PERSPECTIVES

Schiffer Publishing Ltd®

4880 Lower Valley Road, Atglen, Pennsylvania 19310

Written and Photographed
by Scott D. Butcher

# Dedication

For Thomas A. Green and in memory
of Marjorie Elizabeth Green, a true Southern lady.

# Contents

**Other Schiffer Books by Scott D. Butcher**
*Delaware Reflections.* ISBN: 9780764332005. $29.99
*Spooky York, Pennsylvania.* Scott D. Butcher and Dinah Roseberry. ISBN:
    9780764330216. $14.99
*York: America's Historic Crossroads.* ISBN: 9780764330124. $29.99

**Other Schiffer Books on Related Subjects**
*Firestorm at Gettysburg: Civilian Voices June-November 1863.* Jim Slade and
    John Alexander. ISBN: 0764306189. $39.95

Copyright © 2009 by Scott D. Butcher
Library of Congress Control Number: 2009924318

All rights reserved. No part of this work may be reproduced or used in any form or by any means—graphic, electronic, or mechanical, including photocopying or information storage and retrieval systems—without written permission from the publisher.

The scanning, uploading and distribution of this book or any part thereof via the Internet or via any other means without the permission of the publisher is illegal and punishable by law. Please purchase only authorized editions and do not participate in or encourage the electronic piracy of copyrighted materials.

"Schiffer," "Schiffer Publishing Ltd. & Design," and the "Design of pen and ink well" are registered trademarks of Schiffer Publishing Ltd.

Designed by Mark David Bowyer
Type set in Lucian BT / Zurich BT

ISBN: 978-0-7643-3296-8
Printed in China

Schiffer Books are available at special discounts for bulk purchases for sales promotions or premiums. Special editions, including personalized covers, corporate imprints, and excerpts can be created in large quantities for special needs. For more information contact the publisher:

Published by Schiffer Publishing Ltd.
4880 Lower Valley Road
Atglen, PA 19310
Phone: (610) 593-1777; Fax: (610) 593-2002
E-mail: Info@schifferbooks.com

For the largest selection of fine reference books on this and related subjects, please visit our web site at
**www.schifferbooks.com**
We are always looking for people to write books on new and related subjects. If you have an idea for a book please contact us at the above address.

This book may be purchased from the publisher.
Include $5.00 for shipping.
Please try your bookstore first.
You may write for a free catalog.

In Europe, Schiffer books are distributed by
Bushwood Books
6 Marksbury Ave.
Kew Gardens
Surrey TW9 4JF England
Phone: 44 (0) 20 8392 8585; Fax: 44 (0) 20 8392 9876
E-mail: info@bushwoodbooks.co.uk
Website: www.bushwoodbooks.co.uk

# Introduction

The word "Gettysburg" means many things to many different people. To tourists and Civil War buffs, Gettysburg is the site of a pivotal three-day battle that changed the tide of the war. To others, Gettysburg is hallowed ground, a place of over 46,000 casualties, where thousands of soldiers on both sides gave their lives fighting for a cause in which they believed. But Gettysburg is more than the site of a Civil War battle – it is home to two prominent institutions, the Lutheran Theological Seminary at Gettysburg and Gettysburg College. To many people, Gettysburg is a place of learning. And still to others, Gettysburg is a quaint town, a borough that has preserved much of its architecture and exudes a yesteryear charm.

Gettysburg grew from humble beginnings. The first known resident arrived in 1718, and early settlers were primarily Scotch-Irish immigrants. The land that is today Adams County was the "Upper End" of York County until 1800. Samuel Gettys, an early settler, built a tavern in the area that bears his name. In 1786 his son, James, laid out a town with 210 lots centered around a town square. After separating from York County, the new county needed a seat. Several prominent residents of Gettysburg went together to provide free land for the building of a county jail as well as $7000 to be used for construction of a courthouse and administration building. Their efforts were successful, and Gettysburg was named county seat. Adams County is named for President John Adams and was the 26th of 67 Pennsylvania counties. Gettysburg became a borough in 1806.

By the time of the Civil War, Gettysburg's population was 2400, with approximately 450 buildings. The battle that has come to define the town is often characterized as a chance meeting between the Union cavalry and Confederate infantry. The battle that followed involved the 94,000-man Army of the Potomac and 72,000-man Army of Northern Virginia. By the time it was over, approximately 8,000 brave soldiers on both sides lie dead, with another 27,000 wounded, and an additional 11,000 captured or missing.

You can't take more than a few steps in Gettysburg without encountering some aspect of the battle. The Old Dorm on the Lutheran Theological Seminary was a lookout and hospital. Pennsylvania Hall on Gettysburg College was a hospital. Many buildings in and around town were used as shelters, hospitals, or by sharpshooters. Several still bear the scars of the bloody engagement.

But the Borough of Gettysburg also has a quiet charm. Historic buildings surround Lincoln Square, and the streets are lined with well-preserved buildings dating to Gettysburg's early days as a frontier village. The souvenir shops that typically accompany any tourist destination are clustered on Steinwehr Avenue south of Lincoln Square, while a variety of antique shops and boutique stores can be found throughout the borough.

Gettysburg College and the Lutheran Theological Seminary at Gettysburg have spacious campuses with open green space and grand red-brick historic buildings.

Almost two million people visit Gettysburg annually. Unfortunately for some, their experience is limited to the Gettysburg National Military Park, and they never even make it into town to experience the unique ambiance of historic Gettysburg Borough. But for those who do, a treat for the senses awaits.

# Lincoln Square

Lincoln Square has been the heart of Gettysburg since the town was laid out by James Gettys in 1786. Originally known as the "diamond," the town square concept was employed in other central Pennsylvania towns. The square, or diamond, features a circular roundabout that gives Gettysburg its picturesque charm. As the town grew and prospered, businesses clustered around Lincoln Square, and today there are four buildings remaining from the time of the Civil War; the grand Adams County National Bank and Gettysburg Hotel; and several merchants and restaurants.

When Adams County was created from York County in 1800, a court facility for the new county was required. By 1804, a new building stood in the center of the diamond. While today it may seem odd to have a public building in the center of a town square, Adams County was simply following precedent set in Lancaster and York Counties. The square building featured a door on every side. The main floor contained a courtroom and the second floor housed two galleries. In 1859, the courthouse was destroyed by fire and replaced by the building that stands today on Baltimore Street.

**Left:**
The "diamond" has been the heart of Gettysburg since the town was laid out in 1786. Today the diamond is known as Lincoln Square, named in honor of the 16th president, who stayed in a home on the diamond the night before he delivered his three-minute masterpiece, the Gettysburg Address.

## OLD COURTHOUSE

First courthouse for Adams County stood in old Center Square from 1804 to 1859. The land for the Square was given by James Gettys.

PENNSYLVANIA HISTORICAL AND MUSEUM COMMISSION

The Pub & Restaurant on Lincoln Square is a popular destination for locals and visitors alike. The building was destroyed by fire in 2001, but promptly rebuilt to its previous appearance – inside and out.

Adams County National Bank is a prominent building on Lincoln Square. It was constructed in 1906 in the Beaux Arts Classicism style of architecture, which blends Italian Renaissance and Neoclassical features into grand buildings. The stone building was originally home to First National Bank.

*Right:*
The historic Gettysburg Hotel traces its roots to 1797 when James Scott opened a tavern on the diamond. Over the years, a progression of taverns and inns occupied this site, including the Indian Queen Tavern, Franklin House, McClellan Inn, and Hotel Gettysburg. After President Dwight Eisenhower suffered from a heart attack, he headed to his farm in Gettysburg to recuperate. The large hotel served as an operations center. Much of the building was destroyed during a 1983 fire, but it was soon rebuilt. Today, the Gettysburg Hotel is recognized as a Historic Hotel of America, a program of the National Trust for Historic Preservation.

This attractive Federal building on the southeast quadrant of Lincoln Square is known as the Danner House, named for Joel B. Danner. He was a prominent local attorney who acquired the building in 1834. During the time of the battle, Danner used this building as both an office and residence. He also served briefly as a Representative in the U.S. Congress – he was elected to finish the term of the local representative who had died, serving as a congressman for three months.

Built by S.M. Buchman in 1898, the Masonic Building is an interesting study in eclectic Victorian architecture. Perhaps the most prominent feature of the building is a large central Flemish parapet flanked by urn finials. A decorative cornice and red brick lintels give the building texture, while the large second floor windows show a trend toward Commercial Style architecture. A keystone date stone is located in the parapet.

The House of Bender is located in the historic Stoever-Stick Building, which was constructed in 1817. Over the years, the building on the southwest quadrant of Lincoln Square housed a general store, professor's home, and Union hospital. Today, the House of Bender is a purveyor of candles, food products, books, and home accessories.

Antiques, Apples & Art – that's what you'll find at 17 on the Square, located on the northwest quadrant of Lincoln Square. The popular destination houses several tenants, including antique dealers, a winery, and a farm market. The building was constructed in 1807, rebuilt in 1885, and expanded twice in the early twentieth century.

The Company K monument on Lincoln Square recognizes the efforts of Company K of the First Pennsylvania Reserves who fought at Gettysburg. During its existence, the company recruited in Adams County lost 17 men and another 23 were wounded.

This statue, "Return Visit," was created by American sculptor J. Seward Johnson, Jr. and is recognized as one of the most realistic recreations of President Lincoln ever created. It was placed in Lincoln Square in 1991 by the Lincoln Fellowship of Pennsylvania.

One of Gettysburg's most historic buildings is also one of its newest attractions. The David Wills House was the home of a prominent local attorney who was instrumental in the creation of Gettysburg National Cemetery. On November 18, 1863, President Abraham Lincoln arrived at this house and spent the night, putting the final touches on his "brief comments" that came to be known as the Gettysburg Address. Long after the Civil War, Wills continued to be a prominent citizen in Gettysburg. In 1874, he was appointed President Judge. The new David Wills House Museum includes several interpretative galleries, the restored office where Wills coordinated post-battle clean-up efforts, and the bedroom where Lincoln stayed, known as the Lincoln Bedroom. In this picture, painters are "stenciling" brick patterns onto the painted façade.

The Federal building was constructed in 1818 by Colonel Alexander Cobean as a private residence. Five years later, the Bank of Gettysburg purchased the building and leased it to Anthony Kurtz, who established Kurtz's Tavern. David Wills purchased the building in 1854 to serve as both his home and his law office.

During the holiday season, Lincoln Square becomes a festive destination. The tree illuminates on the day of the annual Christmas Parade amid floats, costumed characters, and Christmas carols.

# Around Gettysburg

Much of Gettysburg's charm lies beyond Lincoln Square. Historic buildings, merchants, and restaurants line York Street and Chambersburg Street. High-style late Victorian and early twentieth century houses can be found on Carlisle Street. Several churches can trace their roots to the eighteenth century, and shared a common purpose during and after the battle – that of a makeshift hospital for wounded Union and Confederate soldiers. Several historic educational buildings still stand and have been repurposed for offices or private housing. Two historic railroad stations still exist, and a majestic theater, appropriately named the Majestic Theater, has been given new life through a major restoration and expansion.

Historically known as the Codori House (or Hoke-Codori House), the Brafferton Inn is the oldest continual residence in Gettysburg. The brownstone German colonial building was constructed in 1786 by Michael Hoke, a tanner who worked with the Gettys family. In 1796, it was transferred to his brother, Henry Hoke. Nicholas Codori purchased the home in 1843 and spent much time in the basement with his family during the Battle of Gettysburg. After the battle, Codori allowed his home to be used as a Catholic chapel because of the wounded soldiers still occupying the church. Members of the Codori family lived in the home for 124 years. Today, the property is known as the Brafferton Inn, a bed and breakfast with eighteen guest rooms.

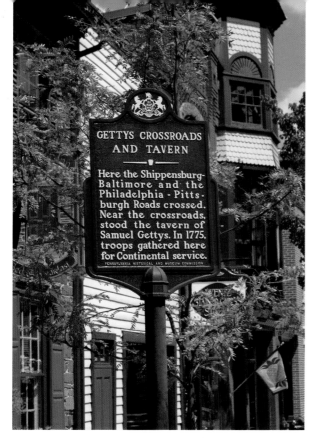

Samuel Gettys was an early settler of the western portion of York County. In 1761, he built a tavern that served as an inn for travelers as well as a meeting place for the nearby settlers. Gettys' son, James, laid out the town twenty-five years later.

John Troxell, Sr. opened the Sign of the Buck Tavern on Chambersburg Street in 1804. By the time of the battle, the building was known as the Union Hotel, though its guests were wounded soldiers. To ready for the 25th anniversary of the battle, the hotel was expanded in 1888 and was then known as the City Hotel. After a period of prosperity, the hotel closed in the 1960s. Fortunately, it was restored and reopened in 1995 as the James Gettys Hotel, named for the founder of Gettysburg. Today, it exhibits its 1920s appearance and is home to twelve suites and Lord Nelson's Gallery.

The Blue Parrot Bistro is located on Chambersburg Street, adjacent to the James Gettys Hotel. Throughout much of the picturesque half-timber building's history, it was known as the Blue Parrot Tea Room. A candy store operated here from the late 1860s until the early twentieth century.

Thaddeus Stevens was born in Vermont in 1792 and moved to York, Pennsylvania, in 1815 to study law and teach. He became an attorney and set up an office in Gettysburg, where he lived from 1816 until 1842, when he relocated to Lancaster. While in Gettysburg, Stevens served in the state legislature. In 1848, he was elected to Congress, where he became known as a radical Republican favoring aggressive action against the Confederate States. Prior to the Battle of Gettysburg, General Jubal Early ordered his men to destroy the Caledonia Iron Works owned by Stevens. After the war, Stevens was instrumental in drafting the Fourteenth Amendment to the U.S. Constitution.

Chambersburg Street west of Lincoln Square includes a number of interesting buildings, retailers, and eateries.

Christ Lutheran Church was founded in 1835 by Samuel Simon Schmucker, who also founded the Lutheran Seminary and Gettysburg College. Of the many sad events that took place during the battle, one of the saddest took place here. Wounded were brought to the church during the fighting on July 1, and Reverend Horatio Howell, a Union chaplain, ministered to them. He stepped onto the porch and was shot dead by a Confederate soldier.

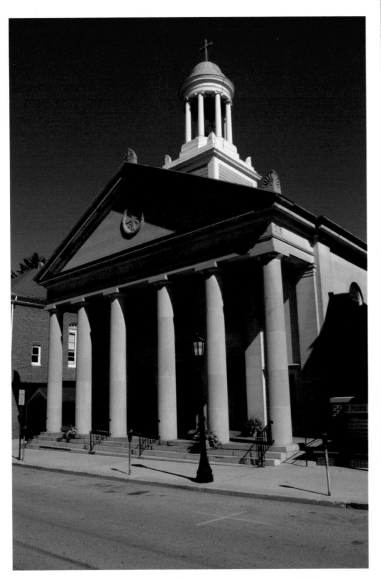

This building was constructed in 1813-1815 to serve as home for the Gettysburg Academy. It has the distinction of being the first home of both the Lutheran Theological Seminary at Gettysburg and Gettysburg College. The Seminary began operations here in 1826 and relocated in 1832. Pennsylvania College, later renamed Gettysburg College, operated here from 1832 until 1837. The building next became a school for young women before becoming a private residence.

St. Francis Xavier Church was dedicated in 1853 and replaced the congregation's first church, which was built in 1831. During the battle, the Sisters of Charity from Emmitsburg, Maryland nursed over 200 seriously wounded soldiers in this building. There were so many wounded that they were laid out on the pews and in the aisles.

In 1800, James Getty donated land upon which a new jail could be located. A two-story stone building with crenellated roofline was constructed in 1803, but burned in 1850. In its place, a new jail was constructed. The building hosted a war council led by Robert E. Lee on July 2, 1863. Twenty-six years later, a third story was added to the front of the building, as were prominent Italianate features. The building operated as a jail until 1949, at which time the Adams County Free Library Association purchased the building and set up a library. In 1991, the Borough of Gettysburg renovated the building to house municipal offices.

The Gettysburg Common School on East High Street was constructed in 1847 and served as a field hospital during and after the battle. There is an account of a Union solider who hid throughout the ordeal in the cupola that once crowned the roof. For over 100 years, the building served as a school, and today it is home to the Adams County Housing Authority.

*17*

This building is the oldest standing church building in the Borough of Gettysburg and was constructed by the local Methodist Episcopalian congregation in 1822. Wounded soldiers were treated here during and after the battle, and in 1874 the congregation relocated to a larger building. The Corporal Johnston H. Skelly Post No. 9 of the Grand Army of the Republic (G.A.R.), a veterans organization, purchased the building in 1880. Over 100 years later, Historic Gettysburg-Adams County, Inc. acquired the building and restored it. The non-profit organization exists to preserve and restore the historic heritage of Adams County's townships and boroughs, with a focus on preservation, interpretation, and welfare of historic, architecturally significant, scenic, and cultural buildings, structures, and sites.

Known as Sheads' Oak Ridge Seminary or Sheads' School for Girls, this home found itself in the middle of the battle on July 1, 1863. Carrie Sheads had planned to send her students home that day, but they were awakened to the sound of war. Retreating Union troops took shelter in the home, and soon it was transformed from school to hospital, with Sheads and her students nursing the wounded. The Confederates advanced, and the hospital fell into their hands. During the fighting, the building was hit by bullets over sixty times.

The Majestic Theater was built in 1925 and was a vaudeville house and silent movie theater in the early days. It was developed by Henry Sharf, owner of the Gettysburg Hotel, from a design by Philadelphia architect W.H. Lee. Today, the Majestic at the Jennifer and David LeVan Performing Arts Center is a community gem, sparkling from a 2005 renovation. The theater has been restored to its 1925 appearance and features a 1200 seat theater while the complex also includes two new cinemas, an art gallery, and the 1950s-themed Mamie's Café.

This building was the home of "Widow" Mary Thompson during the Battle of Gettysburg. It was owned by Thaddeus Stevens and served as Confederate General Robert E. Lee's headquarters. The 1834 house on Buford Avenue was opened to the public as a museum in 1922.

The 100 and 200 blocks of Carlisle Street feature many interesting buildings including several beautiful late Victorian and early twentieth century homes.

One of Gettysburg's most picturesque buildings is the Italianate Gettysburg Railroad Station, which was constructed in 1858-1859. Rail service arrived in the Borough in 1858, and the passenger station was finally completed in May 1859. It was the western terminus of the rail line, so trains had to turn around to head back to Hanover and Hanover Junction, where the tracks intersected with the Northern Central Railway. The station became one of the first field hospitals during the battle, and there is an account of ten to fifteen Union soldiers observing Pickett's Charge from the cupola. After the battle, the station was a hub of activity. Confederates had destroyed bridges and tracks in Adams and York Counties, and residents of both counties worked to restore the tracks to evacuate the wounded. By late July, over 15,000 wounded had been processed through the station.

On November 18, 1863, President Abraham Lincoln arrived at the station then walked to the David Wills House on Lincoln Square. Roughly 24 hours later, after delivering a short address at the dedication of the National Cemetery, Lincoln returned and boarded a train. The last passengers to use the station departed on New Year's Eve day of 1942. The station was restored in 2005-2006, re-opening on the 143rd anniversary of Lincoln's arrival in Gettysburg. Today the historic station houses a museum and is open for tours.

Located on East Middle Street, The Gaslight Inn offers a trip back to the nineteenth century through period furnishings, parlors, a covered deck, and a picturesque garden.

*Left:*
The Gettysburg & Harrisburg Railroad Depot was constructed in 1884 and is today home to Pioneer Lines Scenic Railway. The company operates the Gettysburg Express and features themed excursions including a Ghost Train, Scenic Train, Murder Mystery Dinner, Evening Paradise Dinner, and Santa Train.

Sachs Covered Bridge over Marsh Creek is located on Water Works Road, to the west of the battlefield. It is named for nearby resident John Sachs, whose name has been spelled Sachs, Saucks, and Sochs. The bridge was built in 1854 and is 15-feet wide and 100-feet long. It is believed to have been used by Union troops on the first day of battle, and was then used by retreating Confederate troops after Robert E. Lee decided to leave Pennsylvania. The Army of Northern Virginia is known to have camped near the bridge, and nearby facilities were used as field hospitals.

The Cashtown Inn is located eight miles west of Gettysburg on Old Route 30. It was constructed in 1797, and original innkeeper Peter Marck insisted on cash transactions, creating the nickname Cashtown. Confederate Generals A.P. Hill, Henry Heth, and John Imboden all stopped at the inn, which became headquarters during the occupation. A year earlier, General Jeb Stuart's cavalry had briefly occupied the inn. Today, it serves as a bed and breakfast, restaurant and tavern. In addition to the human occupants, the Cashtown Inn is rumored to be home to spirits from beyond, earning the inn national exposure from shows like Sci-Fi Channel's "Ghost Hunters," which taped an episode here.

The Round Barn and Farm Market is owned and operated by Knouse Fruitlands, Inc. The unique barrel barn is located eight miles west of Gettysburg. It was built in 1914 after the Noah Sheely family's barn was lost in a fire. The barn has a circumference of 282 feet and is over 87 feet in diameter. In 1993, the barn was opened on a limited basis during the National Apple Harvest Festival. Its debut was a success, and one year later regular operating hours were established.

# Gettysburg College & Seminary

Samuel Simon Schmucker was an important part of Gettysburg's early development, founding both the Lutheran Theological Seminary at Gettysburg as well as Gettysburg College, which was originally known as Pennsylvania College. The seminary is the oldest Lutheran seminary in the United States. Over 5,400 students have graduated from the seminary, which educates approximately 270 students at any given time on its historic 52-acre campus. Gettysburg College, a private liberal arts college, was founded in 1832 and today has a sprawling 200-acre campus with over 60 buildings. At any given time there are approximately 2,600 students, who have come from 40 states and 35 countries.

The Abdel Ross Wentz Library at the Lutheran Theological Seminary was constructed in 1947 and renamed in 1965. Today it is home to over 170,000 books, tapes, journals, and microforms.

*Left:*
Schmucker Hall on the campus of the Lutheran Theological Seminary at Gettysburg is better known as the "Old Dorm." It was constructed in 1831-1832 and served many purposes when it originally opened. The building steward was located on the first floor, classrooms on the second floor, and dormitory housing on the third floor. The top floor was meant for future expansion as the seminary grew. On July 1, 1863, Union brigadier general John Buford climbed to the cupola to view the surrounding area and gather intelligence about Confederate troop movements. General John F. Reynolds, who commanded the First Corps of the Army of the Potomac, arrived and provided needed reinforcements. Reynolds also used the cupola to survey the surroundings; however, it would be one of his last actions. He was mortally wounded in the fighting that followed. The building was badly damaged during the battle, and the Confederate Army eventually took possession of it and used the cupola as a signal station. Seminary founder Samuel Simon Schmucker's reputation of being vehemently opposed to slavery was well known, and the Rebel army ransacked the building, pilfering the archives and stripping the furnishings. After the battle, Old Dorm served as a hospital, with 600 wounded soldiers being treated here.

The cupola was destroyed by lightning in 1913. One year later, the "Peace Portico" was erected on the building's west side. For much of the building's life, the main entrance had been on the east side. Students last used the dormitory in 1954. The Federal-style Old Dorm is listed on the National Register of Historic Places and is today home to the Adams County Historical Society. The society exists to identify, preserve, and tell the stories of the people, organizations, businesses, and events that have shaped Adams County.

Valentine Hall on West Confederate Avenue was built in 1894 and named for Milton Valentine, president of the seminary from 1884 to 1903. The building originally contained a library, chapel, classrooms, student rooms, and a gymnasium. Today, the building houses classrooms and offices.

The Church of the
Abiding Presence is the
Seminary Chapel. It was
dedicated in 1942 and
has the distinction of
being the first building
on the campus facing
west. Originally, buildings
were constructed to face
east, but in 1895 West
Confederate Avenue was
constructed to the west,
or rear, of the existing
buildings.

Reverend John A. Singmaster was president of the Lutheran Theological Seminary from 1903 to 1928, and this attractive Colonial Revival building is named for him. It was constructed in 1901 to provide faculty housing. Today it is known as the Singmaster Conference Center, providing accommodations for church groups visiting Gettysburg.

Samuel Simon Schmucker was born in 1799 in Hagerstown, Maryland. His father was a German immigrant and ordained minister. Schmucker was educated at the York Academy, University of Pennsylvania, and Princeton Theological Seminary, then taught at the York Academy. In 1820 he became an ordained Lutheran minister. Schmucker founded the Lutheran Theological Seminary at Gettysburg and Gettysburg College, and was also a noted abolitionist and active agent on the Underground Railroad, using his home and barn to hide fugitive slaves. His home on Seminary Ridge was constructed in 1833 and was damaged during the fighting on July 1, 1863 – both from Union artillery as well as the Confederate soldiers who occupied it. Today it is home to faculty offices and meeting space.

Pennsylvania College was founded in 1832 by Samuel Simon Schmucker, who had founded the nearby Lutheran Seminary in 1826. In 1837 the college moved to Pennsylvania Hall, which was constructed on land donated by Thaddeus Stevens. In 1921, the name of the college changed to Gettysburg College.

Known for many years as the College Edifice, Gettysburg College's Pennsylvania Hall was constructed in 1837 and designed in the Greek Revival style of architecture. It was the first building on the campus, and operated as an instructional facility until 1890, when it was converted into a dorm. It too, for many years, has been called "Old Dorm." The building was renamed Pennsylvania Hall in 1898 and is today an administration building for the college. During the Battle of Gettysburg, the building was primarily used as a Confederate field hospital. General Robert E. Lee is believed to have used the cupola to survey the town and surroundings. Union troops took over the building on July 4, and continued to use it as a hospital. Over 700 wounded soldiers from both sides were treated in the building, which received only minor damage from the battle that raged around it.

Brua Chapel was built in 1890 and named for the parents of Lt. Colonel John P. Brua. Like Glatfelter Hall, Brua Chapel was designed by J.A. Dempwolf in the Victorian Romanesque style. By the 1950s, Gettysburg College had grown enough to make the chapel insufficient to support the needs of the students. A new church was constructed and the building was renamed Brua Hall. Today it houses the college's Theatre Arts program.

Glatfelter Hall on the campus of Gettysburg College was constructed in 1889 for a cost of $92,000. The building was originally known as the Recitation Building and was designed by John Augustus Dempwolf of York, Pennsylvania, who also designed the nearby Brua Chapel and McKnight Hall. The monumental Victorian Romanesque structure features a 143-foot tower, red brick, and brown sandstone trim. In 1912 the building was renamed Glatfelter Hall in honor of P.H. Glatfelter of Spring Grove, Pennsylvania. Glatfelter was both a trustee and benefactor of the college. The building originally housed classrooms, offices, a library, and a museum.

Built in 1898 as a dormitory for men, McKnight Hall today houses the departments of French, German, Italian, and Spanish at Gettysburg College.

Known as the White House, the Norris-Wachob Alumni House has been on the campus of Gettysburg College since 1860. It served as the home for the college president for much of its life. It was renamed for Tom and Joan Wachob Norris, graduates of the college.

Miller Hall, the home of Phi Kappa Psi, was dedicated in 1885. It has the distinction of being the oldest fraternity chapter house in the United States.

Weidensall Hall was built in 1922 and named for Robert Weidensall, a graduate of the college and leader of the local YMCA. The building, which included a swimming pool, was constructed by funds raised by the Woman's League. Today the building houses English, Education, History, Philosophy, and Religion departments.

Breidenbaugh Hall was constructed in 1927 and named for Edward S. Breidenbaugh, an 1868 graduate who headed the chemistry department at Gettysburg College from 1874 to 1924. Today the building is home to Asian Studies and the English Department, as well as the Joseph Theater and the Language Resource Center.

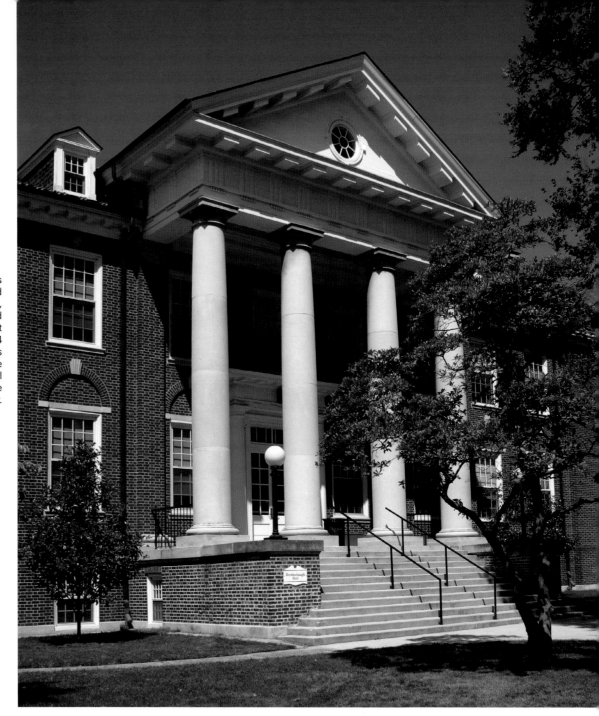

Christ Chapel was built in 1953 to provide a larger venue for campus religious life. The college had grown, and the 1890 Brua Chapel was no longer sufficient. The building was designed by York architect J. Alfred Hamme and built for a cost of $600,000.

Musselman Hall opened in 1958 as a dormitory for women. It is named for Emma G. Musselman who, along with her husband Christian, had a long history of philanthropy in Gettysburg. Today the building serves as a residence hall for upperclassmen.

Stevens Hall is named for attorney Thaddeus Stevens, who donated land for the creation of the Pennsylvania College campus. The building is the fourth oldest building on the campus and today is used for student housing.

Huber Hall was built in 1917 and is one of six residence halls for first year students. It was named for Charles H. Huber, who served as headmaster of Gettysburg Academy and director of the Gettysburg College Women's Division.

After his presidency, Dwight Eisenhower and his wife retired to Gettysburg and the former president became a trustee of Gettysburg College. He was given an office in this building, and it is here that he penned his memoir. Today, the building is known as the Eisenhower House, and is home to the college admissions office.

Located on North Washington Street, the Eisenhower Institute is a non-partisan, non-profit presidential legacy organization. In 1918, Dwight and Mamie Eisenhower spent the summer in this building – the Alpha Tau Omega fraternity. Eisenhower was commanding Camp Colt, the U.S. Army Tank Corps Training Center, which happened to be located on the fields of Pickett's Charge.

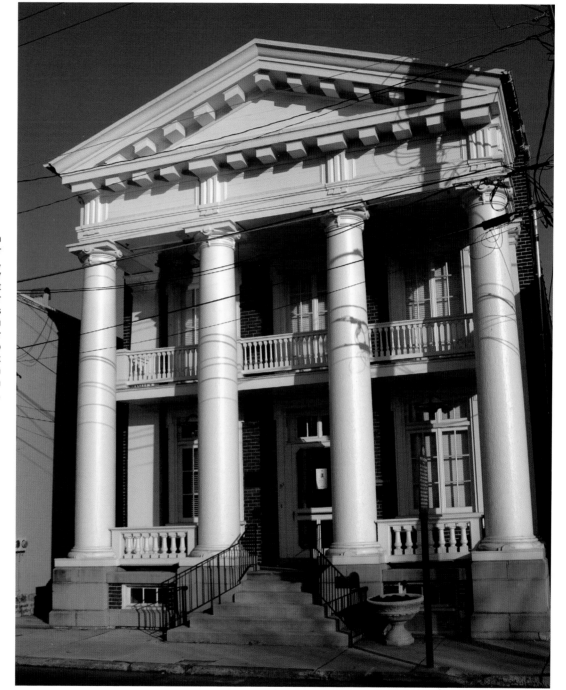

# Steinwehr Avenue, Baltimore Street & Taneytown Road

Steinwehr Avenue is Gettysburg's primary retail district, though stores and restaurants can be found on Baltimore Street, Lincoln Square, and adjacent streets. Several museums are located on Baltimore Pike, near Soldier's National Cemetery, which itself is located between Baltimore Pike and Taneytown Road. Among the retail offerings are antiques, military memorabilia, re-enacting clothing and weapon replicas, and historical art. Several popular restaurants can also be found in the area, as can several historic bed and breakfast inns. This part of town is also a popular stepping off area for the ubiquitous ghost tours that have opened in recent years.

Gettystown Inn has an interesting past. The building in which the bed and breakfast is located was once owned by Lydia Leister; in fact, this two story building once stood adjacent to the Leister House on Taneytown Road, which is better known as General Meade's headquarters. In 1874, Leister constructed a two-story addition to her home. Fourteen years later, she sold her property, including the one-story portion of her house, to the Gettysburg Battlefield Memorial Association. But she liked the two-story addition so much that she had it relocated to the site that it occupies today.

One of the oldest buildings in Adams County is the Reverend Alexander Dobbin House, which was constructed in 1776 when the area was still part of York County. Dobbin used his substantial home as a school of classical learning – one of the first west of the Susquehanna River. He was instrumental in creating Adams County in 1800. During and after the battle, the building was used as a hospital for wounded soldiers. Today the Dobbin House is a destination – a colonial restaurant and tavern in a town known for the Civil War and Victorian architecture.

The Jennie Wade House Museum is actually located at the house of her sister, Georgia Wade. Mary Virginia Wade, or "Ginny" Wade, was at her sister's house during the fighting. A bullet, most likely fired from the Farnsworth Inn building, passed through two wooden doors and struck Ginny, killing her instantly. Her sister continued to bake bread for Union soldiers after the tragedy. At some point after the battle, "Ginny" morphed into "Jennie," the name everyone knows today. She has the distinction as being the only civilian killed during the battle. The house today maintains scars from the war – over 150 bullet holes are present in the Baltimore Street building. The former home is now open as an authentically furnished museum marketed as both a "shrine to a heroic martyr" as well as a "museum of life and living during the American Civil War."

Virginia Wade was born and grew up in this home, which is today the U.S. Christian Commission Museum.

The imposing Adams County Court House was constructed in 1858-1859 from a design by noted Philadelphia architect Stephen D. Button. Architecturally, it blends classical forms with Victorian picturesque architecture. The Italianate style that defines the building was popular in Gettysburg during the mid-nineteenth century. Architect Button also employed Italianate in his design of the Evergreen Cemetery gatehouse. During the initial days of the Army of Northern Virginia's Pennsylvania campaign of 1863, little resistance was encountered. General Jubal Early led his division through Adams County, capturing untrained men from the 26th Pennsylvania Emergency Militia on the way. Early seized the courthouse and eventually paroled the soldiers. During the battle, the courthouse was used as a command post. Like many of the other buildings in Gettysburg, it became a hospital for wounded Union and Confederate soldiers.

The Gettysburg Post Office was completed in 1914 and designed by James Knox Taylor, Supervising Architect of the United States Treasury, the government agency responsible for Federal Government buildings prior to the creation of the General Services Administration. During this period Knox also designed new postal facilities in nearby Hanover and York. The architecture of the Neoclassical building can be described as "high style" because of its many intricate features: bas relief wreaths, egg-and-dart molding, scroll brackets, fluted columns with acanthus capitals, and Greek frets. The building is today home to the Gettysburg Library, a branch of Adams County Library.

The original portion of the Farnsworth House was constructed in 1810, and a large brick addition was built in 1833 by John McFarland. The Sweeney family owned the property during the battle. Confederate sharpshooters took over the house, and it is believed that the bullet that ended the young life of Jennie Wade was fired from the Farnsworth House. Today, over 100 bullet holes are still visible in the exterior walls. In 1972, the building was restored to its 1863 appearance and named in memory of Elon John Farnsworth, a newly promoted brigadier general in the Union Cavalry who died on the third day of the battle.

Gettysburg Presbyterian Church traces its history to 1740 and the establishment of Upper Marsh Creek Presbyterian. The congregation's first building was erected in 1813, and the present location dates from 1842. Like so many other local buildings, it was used as a hospital during and after the battle – originally for the U.S. Cavalry Corps, and then falling into Confederate hands. After delivering his Gettysburg Address, President Abraham Lincoln attended a patriotic meeting at the church; the pew he sat in has been retained and is marked with a plaque. President Dwight D. Eisenhower and his wife, Mamie, were also members of the church.

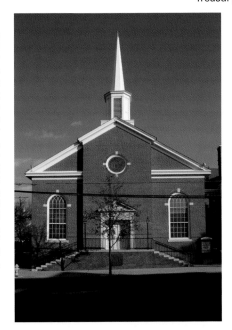

Brickhouse Inn is located on the 400 block of Baltimore Street. The Inn actually includes two buildings – the main Victorian building was constructed by a local banker in 1889 while the adjacent Welty House dates from 1830 and was damaged in the battle. The guest rooms are named for states represented at the Battle of Gettysburg.

In 1860, George Shriver built a brick house on a double lot on Baltimore Street. The new building was both his home and his business – Shriver's Saloon and Ten Pin Alley. At the time of the battle, George Shriver was serving in Cole's Cavalry. His wife, children, and a neighbor's child fled to the Weikert House south of town – little did they know that they would soon be in between the two great armies. Confederate sharpshooters moved in, and two are believed to have been killed in the house. In 1996, the house was restored and reopened as a museum that interprets the effect of the battle on the local civilians.

The Evergreen Cemetery gatehouse was built in 1855 and appears prominently in several photographs taken immediately after the battle. It was the first Italianate building constructed in Gettysburg and was designed by Philadelphia architect Stephen Button. On July 1, 1863, Union Generals Sickles, Howard, and Slocum met at the gatehouse to discuss battle plans. David McConaughy, a prominent local attorney, founded the cemetery and served as its first president. He then helped establish the Gettysburg Battlefield Memorial Association and served as its president for ten years.

Attorney David Wills was instrumental in acquiring land and creating the Gettysburg National Cemetery to relocate Union dead from shallow battlefield graves to a permanent resting place. It was originally known as Soldiers' National Cemetery at Gettysburg. Designed by landscape architect William Saunders, the cemetery features Soldiers' National Monument at the center with graves in semi-circular rows around the monument. The cemetery was dedicated on November 19, 1863, but not completed until 1864 when the last of the 3,512 Union dead were buried. Of that number, 972 are unknown.

The brick Rostrum at Gettysburg National Cemetery was constructed in 1879. A rostrum, by definition, is a stage for public speaking. Three United States presidents have graced this rostrum: Rutherford Hayes, Grover Cleveland, and Theodore Roosevelt.

The main speaker at the dedication of the National Cemetery on November 19, 1863, was Edward Everett. History, however, remembers the three-minute speech by President Abraham Lincoln, who was invited to the dedication by David Wills and asked to give a few remarks. The Lincoln Speech Memorial commemorates that Gettysburg Address. It was dedicated on January 12, 1912, and includes both the invitation from Wills to Lincoln as well as the text of the Address. The bust of Lincoln was sculpted by Henry Kirke Bush-Brown.

Jim Gettys is a well-known Lincoln historian and portrayer. He was a teacher in Ohio in the 1970s, but after growing a beard – and people noticing a striking resemblance to Lincoln – he left teaching and relocated to Gettysburg. Gettys annually portrays Lincoln, reciting the Gettysburg Address at Gettysburg National Cemetery on Remembrance Day. He also offers a general history program as well as a leadership program for corporate executives and managers.

Soldiers' National Monument is the nucleus of the cemetery layout, surrounded by graves in semi-circular rows. It was sculpted in Italy under the direction of Randolph Rogers. The monument contains the "Genius of Liberty" – Lady Liberty with a sword and wreath – as well as four figures representing war, history, plenty, and peace.

The New York State Monument at Gettysburg National Cemetery was dedicated in 1893 in honor of the New York soldiers who fought during the Battle of Gettysburg. More soldiers from New York were wounded or killed than from any other Union state.

The Cyclorama Building has been part of Gettysburg since it was constructed in 1961 as part of the National Park Service's "Mission 66" program to modernize the national parks. It was designed by noted modernist architect Richard Neutra and included a 40-foot high concrete rotunda to house the Battle of Gettysburg Cyclorama, a 360-degree depiction of Pickett's Charge painted by French artist Paul Philippoteaux. The massive painting was completed in 1884, and has been restored and re-exhibited at its new home at the Gettysburg Museum and Visitors Center.

In 1863, John Rupp and his family lived on a home that occupied this site. It was heavily damaged in the battle, and the current building was constructed in 1868. During the first night of the battle, Rupp and his family sheltered in the cellar of the home across the street. The following day, he sent his family across town, and spent the next several days in the home, primarily in the cellar. Today the Rupp House is home to Friends of Gettysburg, part of the Gettysburg Foundation. Their focus is battlefield landscape preservation, land protection, monument restoration, and education, and the Gothic Revival building on Baltimore Street houses interactive exhibits.

The former Visitor's Center for Gettysburg National Military Park was originally known as the Rosensteel Museum, named for the family who had been collecting and preserving artifacts since the smoke cleared in July 1863. In 1921, George Rosensteel opened a museum to display the extensive collection of artifacts related to the Battle of Gettysburg that his uncle John Rosensteel had begun collecting. Ownership was transferred to the National Park Service in 1971. Generations of visitors fondly recall learning about the battle on the Electric Map that was housed within the museum.

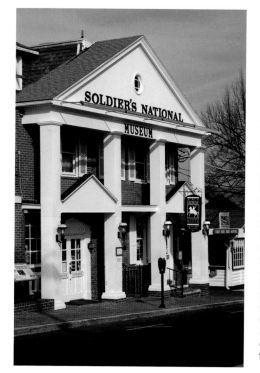

Soldier's National Museum was previously known as the Charlie Weaver Museum of the Civil War and is located in a building that served as the National Soldier's Orphan Homestead until 1877. During the battle, the building served as headquarters for Union general Oliver O. Howard, who's XI Corps were routed by Confederate General Richard Ewell's Corps on the first day of fighting.

The Hall of Presidents on Baltimore Street features reproductions of American presidents "meticulously reproduced in wax in every detail." Visitors also can see reproductions of the Smithsonian Collection of First Ladies Inaugural Gowns as well as an exhibit entitled "Eisenhowers at Gettysburg."

The American Civil War Museum & Gettysburg Gift Center is still frequently called by its former name, the "Wax Museum." The owners promise to bring history back to life through self-guided museum tours and living history programs. At the Battlefield Auditorium, visitors are treated to a life-sized recreation of the Battle of Gettysburg.

"Witness Tree" is a phrase used to describe a tree that witnessed the battle and is still standing. The passage of time and ravages of weather have destroyed most of the Gettysburg witness trees. Twin Sycamores was once home to two of three large sycamore witness trees on Baltimore Street. One of the twin trees is no longer standing. The building itself is called "Twin Sycamores" and reputed to be one of the most haunted sites in Gettysburg.

The George George House on Steinwehr Avenue was home to a Gettysburg laborer. After Major General John F. Reynolds was killed on the battlefield on July 1, his lifeless body was brought to this building. Today, the building is home to Servant's Olde Tyme Photos and a regular stop for the many ghost tours that stroll the streets of town every evening during tourist season.

Among the organizations that regularly offer free living history programs at the American Civil War Museum is the Civil War Heritage Foundation. The non-profit educational organization was founded in 1998 and its members portray historic personalities from the Civil War era. Lancaster County resident G. Edward LeFevre portrays William "Extra Billy" Smith, who was the governor-elect of Virginia while serving as a brigadier general in Jubal Early's division during the battle.

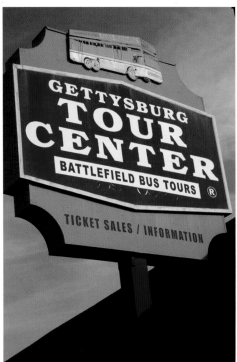

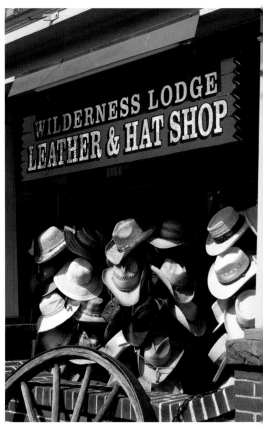

The Lincoln Train Museum is located on Steinwehr Avenue and home to an attraction called the "Lincoln Train Ride," which allows visitors to ride with the 16th president on the Presidential Train en route to Gettysburg. The museum also contains over 1,000 trains, dioramas, and a gift shop with railroad memorabilia.

At the Gettysburg Tour Center guests can chose from one of two tour options. A dramatized audio tour is conducted on double-decker buses while a licensed guide bus tour of the battlefield is available on coach busses.

Wilderness Lodge Leather & Hat Shop offers an assortment of hats, handbags, and leather goods.

9/10/12 ✳

Located in a Victorian building dating from 1860, Habitat is a unique gift shop offering candles, gourmet food, lamps, and home décor.

Greystone Communications Group is a diverse company with several divisions. To Gettysburg visitors, Greystone's American History Store is a popular stop for books, videos, and miniatures. But Greystone actually produces television documentaries, films, and home videos from their facilities in North Hollywood, California. Their retail store in Gettysburg is housed in a building dating from 1880.

Gallon Historical Art features the work of Dale Gallon, who first began painting Civil War scenes in 1980. It became a passion, and he relocated from the West Coast in 1984. Gallon has produced over 200 paintings, some of which have been displayed at the U.S. Army War College in Carlisle, Pennsylvania, and the Pentagon in Washington, D.C.

A sutler is a civilian who sells provisions to an army, or individual soldiers within an army. During the Civil War, sutlers followed both armies, setting up small retail operations adjacent to the camps. Today, sutlers provide reproduction merchandise to reenactors and living historians. The Regimental Quartermaster is a popular Gettysburg sutler. The company was established in 1975 with a goal of providing high quality clothing, goods, and supplies to Civil War reenactors.

At the Gettysburg Quartermaster you'll find military artifacts from the American Revolution through the Vietnam War. The store is part of the Farnsworth Inn complex.

Passages Inn, located on Baltimore Street, is a bed and breakfast inn with a decidedly international theme. Rooms include the European suite, Australasia room, and Africa room, housed in a restored building dating from 1834.

Episcopal services in Gettysburg began in 1867 at the courthouse. The congregation soon moved to a vacated Methodist Church, eventually constructing a new Gothic Revival stone church. The first service of worship was held at the Memorial Church of the Prince of Peace in 1900.

Ghost tours are a popular activity in Gettysburg, with the Ghosts of Gettysburg and Farnsworth House Inn being two of the better-known offerings. Ghosts of Gettysburg, ranked as the top ghost tour in the United States, was created by Mark Nesbitt, a former park ranger, historian, and author of several books of Gettysburg ghost stories. The Farnsworth House Inn offers both Candlelight Ghost Walks as well as the Mourning Theater, which entails ghost stories told in the basement of one of America's most haunted inns.

Dirty Billy's Hats and Abe's Antiques are popular Baltimore Street retailers located south of Lincoln Square. Dirty Billy was a Civil War reenactor who earned the nickname "dirty" because he frequently rubbed dirt from various battlefields onto his reenacting clothing. The store has provided hats for several well-known movies, including *Gettysburg*, *North and South*, *Tombstone*, and *Gods and Generals*.

# Gettysburg National Military Park

The Gettysburg National Military Park was established in 1895. Today the 6,000-acre park is home to almost 1,400 monuments and memorials and is the largest collection of outdoor sculpture in the world. A multi-year restoration project was undertaken to restore the battlefield to its 1863 appearance, enhancing the visitor experience. In May 1863, after defeating the Army of the Potomac in Chancellorsville, Virginia, General Robert E. Lee decided to launch an invasion of the north, his second attempt to do so. Lee's reasons for the invasion, according to his official report, were "the relief of the Shenandoah Valley from the troops that had occupied the lower part of it during the winter and spring, and, if practicable, the transfer of the scene of hostilities north of the Potomac." The battle that ensued in the small borough of Gettysburg involved two great armies and over 160,000 soldiers. With casualties in excess of 46,000, the Battle of Gettysburg ranks as the bloodiest battle on U.S. soil.

The new visitor center at the Gettysburg National Military Park opened in April 2008, promising a "twenty-first century museum experience." Included within the building is the Gettysburg Museum of the American Civil War, which features twelve galleries, eleven of which are based on phrases from Lincoln's Gettysburg Address. Over 300,000 objects and 700,000 archival materials are part of the collection. The $103 million facility also includes a computer resource room, education center, refreshment saloon, and museum bookstore as well as two theaters that show the new film, *A New Birth of Freedom.* The massive building comprises 139,000 sq. ft., including 24,000 sq. ft. of exhibit space.

In September 2008, the restored Gettysburg Cyclorama opened after a five year, $15 million conservation project. The cyclorama was painted by French artist Paul Dominique Philippoteaux and a team of twenty artists. It was not his first Gettysburg Cyclorama. He came to the United States in 1882 and spent several weeks on the battlefield, completing hundreds of sketches. He was further aided by images taken by a local photographer and accounts from veterans who had participated in Pickett's Charge. In total it took approximately a year and a half to complete. The massive painting was exhibited in Chicago in 1883. Due to its success, a second version was painted and exhibited in Boston beginning in 1884. After twenty years, a Gettysburg entrepreneur purchased the canvas, made repairs, and put it on display in a special building constructed on Baltimore Street. It was on display there for forty years before being purchased by the National Park Service in the late 1940s. The cyclorama was relocated to a new building in 1962. The 2003-2008 conservation effort included recreation of missing components of the painting. In 2003, the canvas measured 356-feet by 26-feet; the restored version displayed in 2008 measures 377-feet by 42-feet and weighs 12.5 tons, including backing and hanging systems.

The Eternal Peace Light Memorial was dedicated in 1938 at the 75th anniversary of the Battle of Gettysburg. It is constructed of Alabama limestone and Maine granite and was sculpted by Lee Lawrie.

The Virginia Memorial depicts five soldiers, a young bugler, and a color bearer. It is topped by Robert E. Lee, sitting on his trusty horse, Traveler, and looking toward Cemetery Ridge. Robert Edward Lee was invited in 1861 by President Abraham Lincoln to take command of the Union Army, but he declined and became a military adviser to Confederate States President Jefferson Davis. He took command of the Army of Northern Virginia in 1862 and became General-In-Chief of Confederate Forces in early 1865, only to surrender to Ulysses S. Grant a few months later at Appomattox Court House. After the war he became president of Washington College, which is today known as Washington and Lee University. The monument was sculpted by Frederick William Sievers, who also created statues for the Virginia State Capitol as well as the Stonewall Jackson Monument in Richmond, Virginia.

General George Gordon Meade was a civil engineer and soldier in the Seminole War and Mexican-American War. He worked his way through the ranks and learned on June 28, 1863, that he had been appointed command of the Army of the Potomac to replace General Joseph Hooker. Meade's victory in Gettysburg would be his greatest, though he continued to serve through the end of the war. In March 1864, he became a subordinate to General Ulysses S. Grant. After the war, Meade commanded the Military Division of the Atlantic, Department of the East, and Department of the South. His likeness was sculpted by Henry Kirke Bush-Brown and features Meade on his horse, Old Baldy, who was wounded at Gettysburg, retired, and outlived General Meade by a decade.

The Pennsylvania Memorial is the largest memorial on the battlefield. More than a monument, it is a structure designed in the Beaux Arts Classicism style of architecture. Its dome is topped with the Goddess of Victory and Peace, sculpted by Samuel Murray and made from melted cannons. Giant monoliths depict four battle scenes involving infantry, cavalry, artillery, and the signal corps. Ninety bronze tablets contain 34,500 names – every Pennsylvania soldier who served at the Battle of Gettysburg. Those killed or mortally wounded are marked with a star. The monument was constructed for a cost of $182,000 and dedicated in 1910. In total, 51 designs were submitted, with architect W. Liance Cottrell's design selected. The monument contains 1,252 tons of granite.

The 12, 13, 14, 15, and 16 Vermont Infantry are commemorated in this towering monument, located on Cemetery Ridge along Hancock Avenue. General George J. Stannard commanded the Vermont soldiers, who were principal defenders against Pickett's Charge. Stannard swung out the 13th and 16th Vermont at a 90-degree angle to provide flanking fire, then did the same thing with the 14th and 16th Vermont. These efforts were key to holding the Union Line. The sculpture was created by Karl Gerhardt.

The Codori Farm witnessed Pickett's Charge first hand; in fact, after Pickett emerged from Spangler's Woods to the west, he swung his men around the Codori Farm to assault the Union Center. The original barn is no longer standing. The picturesque structure standing today was constructed in 1884.

The monument to U.S. Regulars on Hancock Avenue near the High Water Mark was erected by the Congress to commemorate the services of the Regular Army in the Gettysburg Campaign. It is 85-feet tall and was dedicated by President William Howard Taft in 1909.

This scene depicts Webb Avenue, near the Copse of Trees, High Water Mark, and The Angle, the name given to a low stone wall that makes an 80-yard right angle turn on Cemetery Ridge. On July 3, 1863, it was defended by General Alexander Webb's Philadelphia Brigade. Pickett's Charge is the name that history has given to an infantry assault ordered by Confederate General Robert E. Lee and carried out, somewhat reluctantly, by General James Longstreet. General Lewis Armistead led his brigade through a gap in the Union line at the Angle, but he fell, mortally wounded. General Winfield Scott Hancock led the Union defense, and was also wounded during the battle. Of the approximately 12,500 Confederates who had stepped out of Spangler's Woods at the beginning of the assault, only 5,000 returned. When fighting on the third day was over, over 4,700 Confederate and 3,150 Union soldiers lie dead on the battlefield.

Jacob Fjelde sculpted this monument to the First Minnesota Infantry to commemorate their heroic actions on July 2, 1863, to protect Cemetery Ridge. They assaulted a much larger force to buy time and allow reinforcements to be brought in. Of the 262 men in the regiment, 215 were casualties. The unwounded survivors helped repulse Pickett's Charge the following day, with another 17 being killed or wounded.

The High Water Mark of the Rebellion Monument was placed at the Copse of Trees in 1892. By definition, a high water mark is the highest level reached by a body of water, so this spot symbolizes perhaps the greatest opportunity that the Confederacy had to win the Civil War. It is not the deepest penetration the Confederates had in Pennsylvania during the war. In the days preceding the battle, Richard Ewell's Corps reached Camp Hill to the north, General Jubal Early's Division occupied York – the largest northern town occupied by the Confederate Army, and General John B. Gordon's Brigade skirmished in Wrightsville, along the Susquehanna River. The High Water Mark in Gettysburg is the site of viscous hand-to-hand combat where Confederate soldiers briefly breached the Union defense. The monument lists the commands of both armies that participated in Pickett's Charge.

The monument to the 12th and 44th New York Infantry atop Little Round Top is one of the most distinctive in the park – a castle-like structure with 44-foot tower and 12-foot square interior chamber. It was designed by General Daniel Butterfield, who served as regimental commander of the 12th New York and first brigade commander of the 44th New York. At Gettysburg he was the Army Chief of Staff, but history perhaps best remembers him as the composer of *Taps*.

Little Round Top is the name given to the smaller of two rocky hills located to the south of Gettysburg. It was the site of a Confederate assault on the Union left during the second day of fighting and defended by Union Colonel Strong Vincent. General Daniel Sickles' III Corps was ordered to defend the southern end of Cemetery Ridge, including Little Round Top; however, he instead moved his troops forward, spreading out from Devil's Den to the Peach Orchard, then northward. Chief Engineer Gouverneur Warren realized that an attack was imminent and sent for help. Major General George Sykes agreed to send the First Division of his V Corps; however, the messenger who carried the order first encountered Col. Vincent, who immediately ordered his four regiments to the defense of Little Round Top without awaiting orders. Almost as soon his men arrived they were under fire from the attacking Confederates.

This curious rock formation on Little Round Top is appropriately named the "Curious Rocks."

This monument to the 155th Pennsylvania Volunteer Infantry was dedicated in 1886. It is topped with the likeness of Samuel W. Hill, a member of Company F who posed for the monument. The 155th Pennsylvania occupied this spot on the second and third day of fighting. While the soldier on the monument is depicted as wearing a Zouave uniform, the 155th Pennsylvania didn't adopt that style uniform until 1864.

The 91st Pennsylvania Infantry monument is one of the most recognizable in the park. It stands on the summit of Little Round Top and is a castellated fortress tower topped with a Maltese Cross, the symbol of the V Corps. This was actually the second monument erected to commemorate the 91st Pennsylvania Infantry and was installed in 1889.

Gouverneur Warren, Chief Engineer of the Army of the Potomac, stood on Little Round Top on July 2, 1863. He requested that a battery positioned in Devil's Den below fire into trees on Seminary Ridge. The sound caused the hidden Confederates to look in the direction of it, and Warren stated that he observed their glistening gun barrels and bayonets, revealing their positions. Warren realized that their battle lines outflanked Union positions, and immediately requested help on Little Round Top. Karl Gerhardt sculpted the monument, which depicts General Warren observing the Confederates along Seminary Ridge.

After a day touring the battlefield, visitors frequently head to Little Round Top to watch another dramatic Adams County sunset.

Located to the west of Little Round Top, Devil's Den is known as much for its unique granite-like rock formations as for its role during the second day of fighting. Devil's Den was the scene of much fighting during General James Longstreet's assault on the Union left, which also included the Wheatfield, Peach Orchard, and Little Round Top. After the Confederates overran Union positions and captured several cannons, Confederate snipers used the protection of the rocks to fire upon Union soldiers on Little Round Top.

Of all the heroic actions that took place during the three days of fighting in Gettysburg, popular culture has all but guaranteed that the actions of Colonel Joshua Lawrence Chamberlain and the 20th Maine remain at the forefront. They were positioned at the end of the Union Line and ordered by Colonel Strong Vincent to hold their position at all costs. For 90 minutes, the 20th Maine, stretched to a single-file line, endured withering attacks from the 15th Alabama. With ammunition running low, Chamberlain ordered a bayonet charge, with the left wing wheeling around to create a simultaneous frontal assault and flanking maneuver. This move held the Union left and resulted in the capture of many Confederates. The movie *Gettysburg*, based on the book *Killer Angels* by Michael Shaara, has helped make this spot one of the most visited on the battlefield. Chamberlain was seriously wounded later in the war and survived, becoming the governor of Maine and later president of Bowdoin College. He received a Medal of Honor in 1893, thirty years after his valiant defense of Little Round Top. The 20th Maine monument was erected in 1886 and commemorates the 38 Maine soldiers who died.

The Tennessee Memorial was designed by Felix deWeldon, best known for sculpting the Iwo Jima Memorial in Arlington, Virginia. The monument was originally to have 3-dimensional bronze figures, a design that is etched on the face of the memorial. Felix deWeldon has the distinction of being the only artist in the world to have a sculpture placed on all seven continents.

Dedicated in 1929, the North Carolina Memorial was one of the earliest state memorials at Gettysburg. The bronze statue was sculpted by Gutzon Borglum, best known for his work at Mount Rushmore. The statue depicts five soldiers, with a wounded officer urging his men forward. The monument stands at the general location that General James Pettigrew emerged from the woods, leading a brigade of North Carolinians on July 3 in the assault that became known as Pickett's Charge.

Lieutenant General James Longstreet, General Lee's "Old War Horse," was a corps commander in the Army of Northern Virginia. History remembers him for disagreeing with Lee's strategy at Gettysburg; however, he was also Lee's primary general after the death of Thomas Jonathan "Stonewall" Jackson at Chancellorsville, Virginia. Longstreet's corps had great success on the second day of fighting in Gettysburg; however, they were unable to dislodge the Union from their positions on Cemetery Ridge. After Gettysburg, Longstreet transferred to the Western Theater, rejoining the Army of Northern Virginia for the Battle of the Wilderness. After the war he served in many political positions, including U.S. Ambassador to the Ottoman Empire and U.S. Commissioner of Railroads.

Dedicated in 1971, the Louisiana Memorial is one of the more interesting statues on the battlefield. It was sculpted by Donald DeLue and features a fallen soldier clutching a flag. Above him the Spirit of the Confederacy rises, holding a flaming cannonball and blowing taps for the fallen soldiers. DeLue also sculpted the nearby Mississippi Memorial as well as the Omaha Beach Memorial in Normandy, France.

The Mississippi Memorial was dedicated in 1973 and sculpted by Donald DeLue. General William Barksdale led a Mississippi brigade from this spot, successfully attacking Union forces in the Peach Orchard. The statue depicts two soldiers – one has fallen, and the other is defending the fallen colors.

The Longstreet Tower on West Confederate Avenue is one of five towers erected on the battlefield by the War Department. Two other towers remain – one on Culp's Hill, and one on Oak Ridge. The latter tower was eventually shortened. Towers on Big Round Top and at the site of the Cyclorama Building were eventually dismantled.

The Peach Orchard was the location of Union defenses on the second day of the Battle of Gettysburg. The Union line stretched from Devil's Den to the Peach Orchard, then northward along Emmitsburg Road. Like other locations in the Valley of Death, the Peach Orchard was eventually overrun by the Confederates – in this case General Lafayette McLaws' Division.

The Wheatfield was the scene of horrific fighting on July 2, 1863. When the smoke cleared, over 4,000 Confederate and Union soldiers had been killed or wounded. During the assault, the Wheatfield changed hands six times.

This bank barn along Plum Run was owned by Abraham Trostle during the Battle of Gettysburg. On July 2, the family was warned that they were in imminent danger, and they wisely fled. General Daniel Sickles coordinated his corps from the property until being seriously wounded by a Confederate shell. As he was carried away on a stretcher, he insisted on lighting a cigar and continuing to rally his men. He eventually lost his leg, and the Trostle Farm was overrun by the Mississippi Infantry.

The unassuming Lydia Leister House served as General Meade's headquarters and was the location of a Council of War on the second day of the battle. Officers in attendance were asked three questions: 1. Should the Union Army remain in Gettysburg? 2. Should they wait for General Lee to attack, or attack him first? 3. If they wait for his attack, how long should they wait before launching an assault on the Confederate Army? A decision was made to shore up weaknesses in defenses and wait another day for Lee to attack.

*Left:*
The picturesque George Weikert House was located in the path of the Confederate advance on July 2, with horrific fighting taking place to the west at the Peach Orchard and south at Little Round Top.

This picturesque view was taken along Slocum Avenue at Culp's Hill, which was an important part of the Union's defensive line. The right flank has been called the fishhook. General Richard Ewell was ordered to take Culp's Hill on the first day of fighting, but he did not attack. Ewell began an artillery barrage during the late afternoon of the second day of fighting, launching an infantry assault toward evening, making some advances and taking positions previously held by Union defenders. The fighting lasted until close to midnight. The Army of the Potomac was able to reinforce their positions overnight, unleashing an artillery assault in the early morning hours. During the fighting that ensued, the Union troops were able to repel the Confederates and take back the positions that they had lost a day earlier. The Confederates retreated across Rock Creek.

*Left:*
Spangler's Spring provided fresh water to soldiers on both sides of the battle. Located at the southern end of Culp's Hill, it was the location of a Confederate assault on the second day. The Confederates occupied the lower slopes of the hill as a result. On the third day, seven hours of fighting ensued as the Union Army sought to dislodge the Confederate Army from their positions.

This sunrise photograph was taken from Emmitsburg Road, looking toward the Angle and Copse of Trees.

General Winfield Scott Hancock was born in Montgomery Square, Pennsylvania, and wounded at Gettysburg. He served as commander of the Union II Corps, which bore the brunt of Pickett's Charge. Hancock made himself an easy target during the assault, rallying his men on horseback despite pleas that he dismount from his horse. After being wounded, he refused to be evacuated to a hospital until the battle was decided. After the war, Hancock supervised the executions of John Wilkes Booth's co-conspirators and became the Democratic candidate for President of the United States, losing to James Garfield by only 10,000 votes.

Oliver O. Howard almost became a minister before the Civil War. At Fair Oaks, he was wounded and lost his right arm. Howard commanded the XI Corps at Gettysburg and was routed by Confederate General Richard Ewell's Corps on the first day of fighting. He was sent to the Western Theater, where he had great success and became Commander of the Army of the Tennessee. After the war he became superintendent of the U.S. Military Academy at West Point and was instrumental in the creation of Howard University, which bears his name.

# Bibliography

## Books

Hartwig, D. Scott and Ann Marie. *Gettysburg – The Complete Pictorial of Battlefield Monuments*. Gettysburg, PA: Thomas Publications, 1988, 1995.

Herzon, Kate. *Insiders' Guide to Gettysburg*. Guilford, CT: Morris Book Publishing, LLC, 2006.

TravelBrains. *Gettysburg Expedition Guide: The Complete Gettysburg Experience*. United States: TravelBrains, Inc., 2000.

## Pamphlets and Unpublished Works

Gettysburg Convention and Visitors Bureau. "Gettysburg 2008 Official Visitors Guide." Harrisburg, PA: Advanced Communications, 2008.

"Gettysburg National Military Park." National Park Service, U.S. Department of the Interior, Reprint 2008.

"National Register of Historic Places Inventory – Nomination Form, Gettysburg Battlefield Historic District." 1985.

Pennsylvania Register of Historic Sites and Landmarks. "National Register of Historic Places Inventory – Nomination Form, Old Dorm – Gettysburg College." Harrisburg, PA: Pennsylvania Historical and Museum Commission, 1971.

Sherfy, Marcella M. "National Register of Historic Places Inventory – Nomination Form, Dobbin House." Gettysburg, PA: Gettysburg National Military Park National Park Service, 1972.

Sickles, Eugene S. and David M. Berman. "National Register of Historic Places Inventory – Nomination Form, Adams County Courthouse." Gettysburg, PA: Pennsylvania Historical and Museum Commission, 1974.

Smith, Janet C. "National Register of Historic Places Inventory – Nomination Form, Old Dorm – Lutheran Theological Seminary." Harrisburg, PA: Pennsylvania Historical and Museum Commission, 1973.

Zacher, Susan M. "Covered Bridges of Adams, Cumberland, and Perry Counties TR." Harrisburg, PA: Pennsylvania Historical and Museum Commission, 1980.

## Web Sites

http://155thpa.tripod.com
http://cwhfinc.org
http://kevintrostle.com
http://milvet.state.pa.us
http://puka.cs.waikato.ac.nz
http://siris-artinventories.si.edu
www.17onthesquare.com
www.achs-pa.org
www.adamslibrary.org
www.brafferton.com
www.brickhouseinn.com
www.cashtowninn.com
www.civilwarheadquarters.com
www.civilwarhome.com
www.civilwarnews.com
www.dobbinhouse.com
www.eisenhowerinstitute.org
www.emmitsburg.net
www.evergreencemetery.org
www.farnsworthhouseinn.com
www.friendsofgettysburg.org
www.gallon.com

www.gettysburg.com
www.gettysburg.edu
www.gettysburg.stonesentinels.com
www.gettysburg.travel
www.gettysburgbattlefieldtours.com
www.gettysburgdaily.com
www.gettysburgepiscopal.org
www.gettysburgmuseum.com
www.gettysburg-pa.gov
www.gettysburgpa.org
www.gettysburgpresbyterian.org
www.gettysburgrail.com
www.gettysburgtourguides.org
www.greystoneonline.com
www.hallowedground.org
www.hotelgettysburg.com
www.jennie-wade-house.com
www.livingplaces.com

www.loc.gov
www.ltsg.edu
www.macungie.org
www.mainstreetgettysburg.org
www.mission66.com
www.nps.gov
www.nytimes.com
www.passagesinngettysburg.com
www.phmc.state.pa.us
www.roundbarngettysburg.com
www.ss-sutler.com
www.tbhabitat.com
www.thegaslightinn.com
www.the-pub.com
www.usccgettysburg.org
www.virtualtourist.com
www.whtm.com
www.wikipedia.org